THE HISTORY OF FOODS

# FROZEN TREATS

by Kristine Spanier, MLIS

## Ideas for Parents and Teachers

Pogo Books let children practice reading informational text while introducing them to nonfiction features such as headings, labels, sidebars, maps, and diagrams, as well as a table of contents, glossary, and index.

Carefully leveled text with a strong photo match offers early fluent readers the support they need to succeed.

### Before Reading

- "Walk" through the book and point out the various nonfiction features. Ask the student what purpose each feature serves.
- Look at the glossary together. Read and discuss the words.

### During Reading

- Have the child read the book independently.
- Invite them to list questions that arise from reading.

### After Reading

- Discuss the child's questions. Talk about how they might find answers to those questions.
- Prompt the child to think more. Ask: Were you surprised to learn that a child invented Popsicles?

Pogo Books are published by Jump!
3500 American Blvd W, Suite 150
Bloomington, MN 55431
www.jumplibrary.com

Copyright © 2026 Jump! International copyright reserved in all countries. No part of this book may be reproduced in any form without written permission from the publisher.

Jump! is a division of FlutterBee Education Group.

Library of Congress Cataloging-in-Publication Data

Names: Spanler, Kristine, author.
Title: Frozen treats / by Kristine Spanier, MLIS.
Description: Minneapolis, MN: Jump!, Inc., [2026]
Series: The history of foods | Includes index.
Audience: Ages 7-10
Identifiers: LCCN 2024055962 (print)
LCCN 2024055963 (ebook)
ISBN 9798892139151 (hardcover)
ISBN 9798892139168 (paperback)
ISBN 9798892139175 (ebook)
Subjects: LCSH: Ice cream, ices, etc. –History–Juvenile literature. | Inventors–History–Juvenile literature.
Classification: LCC TX795 .S625 2026 (print)
LCC TX795 (ebook)
DDC 641.86209–dc23/eng/20241205
LC record available at https://lccn.loc.gov/2024055962
LC ebook record available at https://lccn.loc.gov/2024055963

Editor: Jenna Gleisner
Designer: Molly Ballanger

Photo Credits: unpict/Shutterstock, cover; Andrei Kuzmik/Shutterstock, 1; Kellis/Shutterstock, 3; M. Unal Ozmen/Shutterstock, 4; Su Nitram/iStock, 5 (foreground); robypangy/iStock, 5 (background); Kristini/Shutterstock, 6; Historic Collection/Alamy, 6-7; John Vachon/Library of Congress, 8-9; P Maxwell Photography/Shutterstock, 9; p.studio66/Shutterstock, 10; adsR/Alamy, 11 (foreground); vulcano/Shutterstock, 11 (background); Martha McMillan Roberts/Library of Congress, 12-13; Ari Perilstein/Getty, 14-15; Peter Sickles/SuperStock, 16; Rosalie Che/Shutterstock, 17 (foreground); Lester Balajadia/Shutterstock, 17 (background); Angela Rowlings/MediaNews Group/Boston Herald/Getty, 18-19; StockImageFactory/Shutterstock, 20-21 (foreground); Pla2na/Shutterstock, 20-21 (background); RadioActive/Wikimedia, 23.

Printed in the United States of America at Corporate Graphics in North Mankato, Minnesota.

# TABLE OF CONTENTS

**CHAPTER 1**
Ice Cream Inventions............................4

**CHAPTER 2**
Popsicles and More............................10

**CHAPTER 3**
Ice Cream Shops............................16

**QUICK FACTS & TOOLS**
Timeline............................22
Glossary............................23
Index............................24
To Learn More............................24

# CHAPTER 1

# ICE CREAM INVENTIONS

Do you love ice cream? In 1744, the governor of Maryland had a party. He served ice cream. One of his guests wrote about the treat. This is the first **record** of ice cream in America!

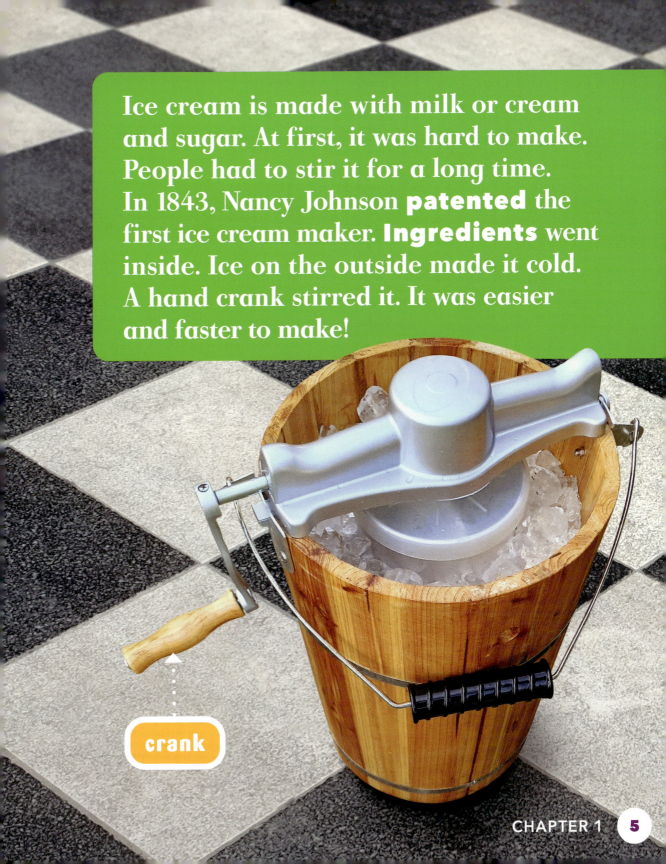

Ice cream is made with milk or cream and sugar. At first, it was hard to make. People had to stir it for a long time. In 1843, Nancy Johnson **patented** the first ice cream maker. **Ingredients** went inside. Ice on the outside made it cold. A hand crank stirred it. It was easier and faster to make!

crank

People in the United States first ate ice cream on plates. They used tiny spoons. That changed at the **World's Fair** in 1904. It was in St. Louis, Missouri. Ice cream was sold in curled waffle cookie cones. Why? People could hold it in one hand and walk while they enjoyed the fair. This was how ice cream cones were **invented**!

waffle cone

CHAPTER 1

1904 World's Fair

CHAPTER 1

soda fountain

CHAPTER 1

In 1904, David Strickler worked at a **soda fountain**. He sold ice cream treats. One day, he cut a banana the long way. He put three scoops of ice cream on top. He covered them with **toppings**. He invented the banana split!

### WHAT DO YOU THINK?

The ice cream sundae was invented in the 1880s. A sundae can have any **syrups** and other toppings. If you could build an ice cream sundae, what would you put on it? Why?

banana split

CHAPTER 1  9

## CHAPTER 2
# POPSICLES AND MORE

Did you know a kid invented Popsicles? In 1905, Frank Epperson was 11 years old. One night, he left a soda outside with a stir stick in it. It was frozen in the morning! He tasted it. He thought it was great.

Epperson patented his creation in 1924. First, it was called an Epsicle. He later changed the name to Popsicle.

CHAPTER 2

IT'S PURE CREAM
SPECIAL
Brimers
15¢ PINTS
ALL FLAVORS
BUY THEM HERE
ICE CREAM
HERE
TRADE MARK REG. U.S. PAT. OFF.

Around the same time, the Good Humor company created an ice cream treat. It was covered in chocolate. The company had trucks with freezers. The trucks had bells. Drivers rang them. Children could hear them. They knew ice cream was on the way. Ice cream trucks were born!

I.C. and J.T. Parker were brothers. In 1928, they had an idea. It was for a new **prepackaged** ice cream cone treat. But ice cream made the cones soggy. They talked to **food scientists**. They learned to put chocolate on the inside of the cone. The ice cream didn't touch it. This was how the Drumstick was created!

### DID YOU KNOW?

By the 1940s, larger freezers were added to refrigerators. People had extra room for frozen food. More companies began selling frozen treats. People could enjoy more treats at home!

CHAPTER 2 15

# CHAPTER 3
# ICE CREAM SHOPS

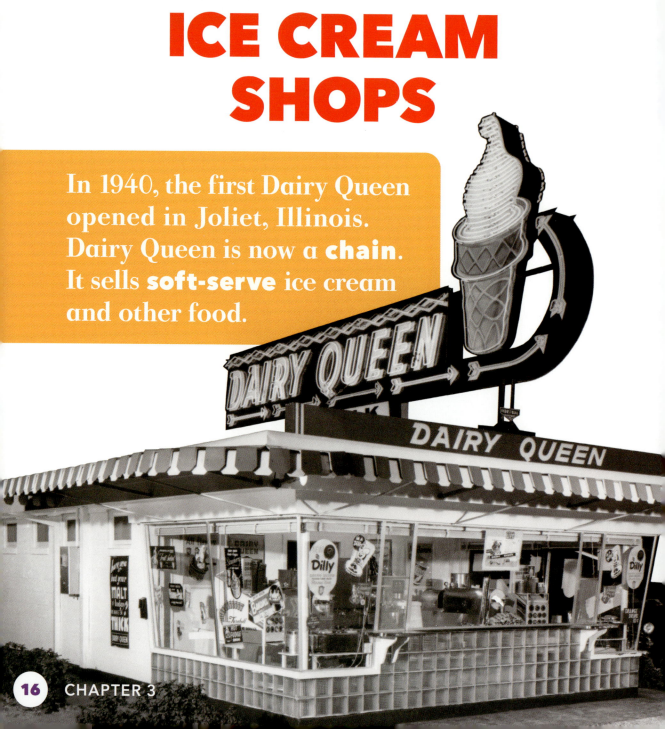

In 1940, the first Dairy Queen opened in Joliet, Illinois. Dairy Queen is now a **chain**. It sells **soft-serve** ice cream and other food.

Samuel Temperato owned many Dairy Queens in Missouri. He invented the Blizzard in 1985. A Blizzard is a thick shake. It has candy and other treats in it.

CHAPTER 3   **17**

Baskin-Robbins opened in Glendale, California, in 1945. It is known for having 31 ice cream **flavors**. "31" is even part of the **logo**!

logo

# TAKE A LOOK!

What are the top 10 most popular ice cream flavors? Take a look!

1. VANILLA
2. CHOCOLATE
3. STRAWBERRY
4. BUTTER PECAN
5. COOKIE DOUGH
6. COOKIES AND CREAM
7. MINT CHOCOLATE CHIP
8. CHOCOLATE CHIP
9. ROCKY ROAD
10. PEANUT BUTTER

CHAPTER 3

We can buy frozen treats in restaurants. We can buy them at stores, too. There are so many kinds and flavors to enjoy. What would you like to try next?

## WHAT DO YOU THINK?

Why do you think people love frozen treats? What frozen treat would you invent? Why?

CHAPTER 3

# QUICK FACTS & TOOLS

## TIMELINE

Take a look at some important dates in the history of frozen treats!

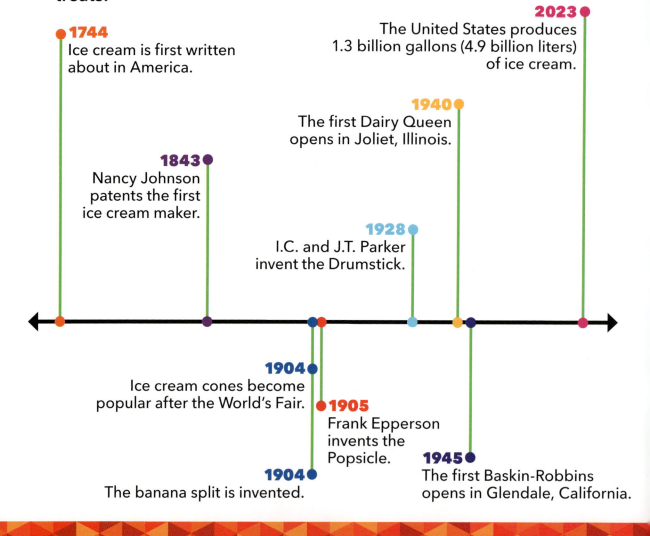

**1744** Ice cream is first written about in America.

**1843** Nancy Johnson patents the first ice cream maker.

**1904** Ice cream cones become popular after the World's Fair.

**1904** The banana split is invented.

**1905** Frank Epperson invents the Popsicle.

**1928** I.C. and J.T. Parker invent the Drumstick.

**1940** The first Dairy Queen opens in Joliet, Illinois.

**1945** The first Baskin-Robbins opens in Glendale, California.

**2023** The United States produces 1.3 billion gallons (4.9 billion liters) of ice cream.

# GLOSSARY

**chain:** A group of restaurants owned by the same company that offers the same menu items.

**flavors:** Tastes.

**food scientists:** People who use chemistry, biology, and other sciences to study the basic elements of food.

**ingredients:** Items used to make something.

**invented:** Created and produced for the first time.

**logo:** A symbol that stands for a company.

**patented:** Got a legal document that gives the inventor of an item the sole rights to manufacture or sell it.

**prepackaged:** Wrapped and packed before being sold.

**record:** The facts about something that has occurred.

**soda fountain:** The equipment and counter for the preparation and serving of sodas, sundaes, and ice cream.

**soft-serve:** Smooth, soft ice cream that is made in and dispensed from a freezer in which it is continuously stirred.

**syrups:** Thick, sweet liquids made by boiling sugar and water, usually with flavoring.

**toppings:** Things placed on top of a food to add flavor or decoration.

**World's Fair:** An international exposition featuring exhibits from all over the world.

## INDEX

banana split 9
Baskin-Robbins 18
Blizzard 17
Dairy Queen 16, 17
Drumstick 14
Epperson, Frank 10, 11
flavors 18, 19, 20
food scientists 14
freezers 13, 14
Good Humor 13
ice cream cones 6, 14
ice cream maker 5
ice cream trucks 13
ingredients 5
Johnson, Nancy 5
logo 18
Parker brothers 14
Popsicles 10, 11
soda fountain 9
soft-serve ice cream 16
Strickler, David 9
sundae 9
Temperato, Samuel 17
toppings 9

## TO LEARN MORE

**Finding more information is as easy as 1, 2, 3.**

❶ Go to www.factsurfer.com
❷ Enter "frozentreats" into the search box.
❸ Choose your book to see a list of websites.

24  QUICK FACTS & TOOLS